Britannica's

5-Minute

Really True
Stories for Family Time

Britannica's
5-
Minute
Really True
Stories for Family Time

BRITANNICA
BOOKS

Contents

No Place Like Home

Home is different for everyone. It can be a brick house standing in a row, a mobile home, or a bungalow. Home can be on a farm or floating on a canal. It can be in a tent, a treehouse, or even underground. There are billions of homes around the world with families gathered inside. Shall we visit a few?

First stop, an apartment building! Concrete apartment buildings were first built by the ancient Romans. They needed to build homes upward and make room for more people to live in the same space. Today, tall apartment buildings are found all over the world. They come in many shapes, sizes, and colors. Some have balconies for hanging out the laundry, potting plants, or just relaxing. Others have courtyards where people can sit and chat with neighbors and children can play. One huge complex of five apartment buildings in Hong Kong is called the Monster Building. It contains 2,243 homes!

Chickens eat grains and worms.

Sheep like to munch on grass and other leafy plants.

Donkeys and cows graze on grass and hay.

In the countryside, there is more open space. This is where we usually find farmhouses. Some farmers and their families care for animals, such as chickens, cows, goats, and sheep. Others grow food, such as corn, rice, and wheat. Some farmers might do both. A farmer's day is long and busy. After school, the children might help with tasks like feeding the animals. When their day is done, the family heads indoors for dinner and bedtime.

People live all over the world, even in places with extreme weather. In the scorching desert of southern Australia, there is a small town called Coober Pedy. Here, people have come up with a clever solution to avoid the heat. They build their homes underground, where the temperature stays nice and cool. The walls, hallways, and even bookshelves in these homes are all carved out of rock.

Unlike the dry Australian desert, the country of Bangladesh has lots of water. It sits in the world's largest delta, which is a low-lying plain created by a river as it flows out toward the sea. In the rainy season, the rivers in the area overflow and flood the surrounding land. To protect their houses from the water, some families have built their homes on raised mud mounds. In some parts of the country there are even floating schools.

Some houses have grass growing on their roofs! These are a type of eco, or planet-friendly, home. Around the world, people are building eco homes to save energy and help protect the environment. These green roofs keep warm air inside the house when it is cold outside, and cool air inside when it is hot outside. Less fuel needs to be burned for heating and cooling, which saves energy. Green roofs also improve the quality of the air by soaking up a gas called carbon dioxide, and releasing oxygen, which is the gas that humans breathe in.

Another type of eco home, called an Earthship, was first built in the 1970s in New Mexico. The walls are made from recycled materials such as bottles, aluminum cans, or old tires filled with soil. Solar panels on the roofs absorb sunlight and use its power to make electricity. Some Earthships also include a composting toilet. These toilets don't need water. They just need the right temperature, moisture, and bacteria to turn human waste into compost. Then, the compost can be used to grow plants in the yard.

What do you imagine your home might look like in the future?

What's for Breakfast?

Before you open your eyes in the morning, you might hear your family rattling around in the kitchen. As you peek through your eyelids, your tummy rumbles. You realize you're hungry. It's time for breakfast! You jump out of bed and head to the kitchen.

In different parts of the world, people eat different things for breakfast. Kids waking up in Ethiopia look forward to eating a bowl of *genfo* (GUN-foe). *Genfo* is a type of hot cereal made from barley or wheat cooked with milk or water.

A family will usually share one big bowl of steaming *genfo*. It is placed in the middle of the table so that everyone can reach it. The *genfo* will often have delicious butter flavored with spices in the center.

Using either a spoonlike stick or, more often, just their fingertips, each family member will reach into the bowl and scoop up a bite-sized ball of hot *genfo*. They can then dip it into the spicy butter and pop it into their mouths. Yum!

Kids in Iceland eat a different kind of hot cereal, which they call *hafragrautur* (HA-vra-grey-tur). They might top it with milk, brown sugar, butter, or raisins.

In Mexico, many families enjoy *chilaquiles* (chee-la-KEY-lays) for breakfast. This dish is made with fried corn tortillas covered with a special tomato sauce. Cheese, cream, and onion are then added to the top. Eggs or refried beans are popular side dishes. Breakfast is served!

In England, a traditional breakfast is called a full English, or a fry-up. It includes eggs, bacon, sausages, baked beans, hash browns, tomatoes, and toast. This meal dates back to the 1300s. At that time, it was the breakfast of the wealthy. Most other people could afford only hot cereal or bread.

For breakfast in Japan everyone usually has a combination of small dishes. These include rice mixed with salmon eggs, called *ikura* (ee-ku-ra), or sea urchin, called *uni* (oo-nee). Add some eggs sprinkled with *furikake* (foo-ree-ka-kay), which is a mixture of dried fish, seaweed, sesame seeds, and flavorings, and you have a delicious breakfast. Sometimes, a salad made of pickled vegetables is included, too.

Sometimes, families have to eat a quick breakfast on the move as they travel to school or work. In France, it's common to eat croissants (kwah-SAHNTS), which are buttery, flaky pastries shaped like crescent moons. But these tasty treats can leave a trail of crumbs, so be sure to grab a napkin before you dash out the door.

In Montréal, Canada, bagel shops are very popular. A bagel is a bread roll that is shaped like a doughnut and has been both boiled and baked. What makes Montréal bagels unique is that they are often boiled in honey water and then baked in a wood-burning oven. This gives them a sweet flavor and crisp crust. Like croissants, bagels are a quick breakfast and are easy to eat on the go.

In China, many people get their food-on-the-go from street vendors. Sweet, deep-fried dough sticks, called *youtiao* (yoh-tyaow), with a cup of soy milk is a popular, quick breakfast. Dipping the dough sticks into the soy milk is highly recommended! Steamed buns are another favorite in China. These buns, called *baozi* (bow-tsuh), are sometimes savory and sometimes sweet. Savory buns have meat and vegetables inside, whereas the sweet buns are stuffed with a combination of bean paste, custard, sesame seeds, and sugar.

Now that you've read about a variety of tasty breakfasts from around the world, which one would you most like to eat?

Staying Clean

"Lunchtime! Please wash your hands before you come to the table!" Have you heard this call when you're playing outside? After running around, you might be feeling hungry and would rather go straight to the table instead of washing your hands. But maybe they *are* dirty after digging in the dirt, climbing trees, and throwing balls for the dog! So, off to the sink you go.

You turn on the tap and stick your hands under the running water. Then you rub them together and figure you're done. But when you look at your hands, they're still dirty! So you try again, this time using soap. Much better! Off you go to join your family for lunch. It smells delicious!

Splish! Splash!

What is it about soap that makes it so important for cleaning your hands—and the rest of your body? Why can't you get clean with only water? Let's take a look at the science of soap.

People invented soap more than 4,000 years ago. They made it by boiling animal fat with ashes from their cooking fire. The ashes contained a chemical called an alkali, which reacts with fat to make soap. People still make soap by heating fat with an alkali today.

Soap is made up of chains of tiny structures called molecules that you can only see through a microscope. One end of each chain sticks to oil and dirt. The other end of each chain sticks to water.

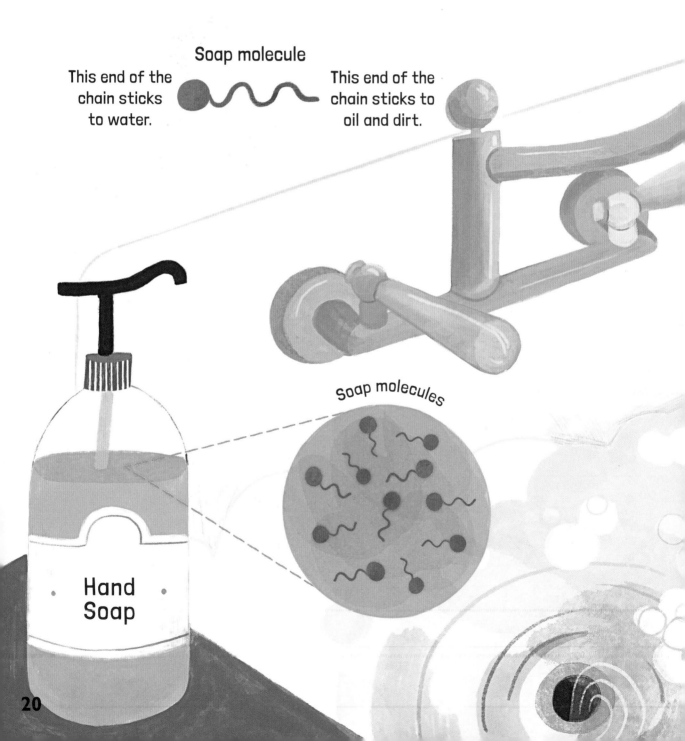

Soap molecule

This end of the chain sticks to water.

This end of the chain sticks to oil and dirt.

Soap molecules

Hand Soap

As you rub your hands together to make a bubbly lather, the soap begins to do its job. One end of the soap chains sticks to any oil, grease, or dirt on your hands. The other end clings to the water as you rinse. Then, *swoosh*...the water, soap, and dirt are washed down the drain!

So, this is why you need water *and* soap to wash your hands properly: one doesn't work without the other. Now let's learn the best method for getting your hands squeaky clean.

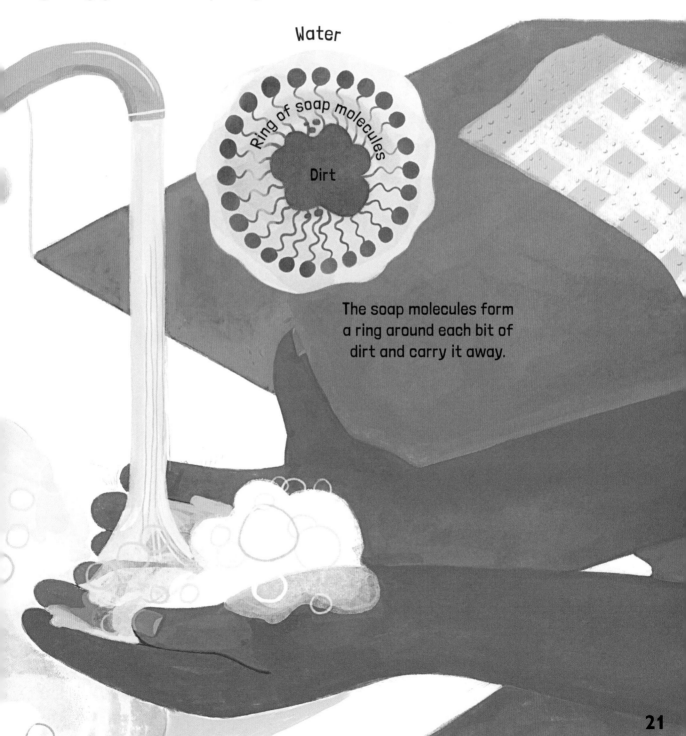

Water

Ring of soap molecules

Dirt

The soap molecules form a ring around each bit of dirt and carry it away.

In order to get your hands truly clean, you need to wash them for long enough and in a particular way. Here is how to wash your hands properly:

1.
Wet your hands.

2.
Use enough soap to completely cover your hands.

3.
Rub your hands, palm to palm.

4.
Put one palm on top of your other hand. Lace your fingers together and rub up and down between them. Make sure you're also rubbing the back of your hand. Do the same with the other hand.

5.
Put your palms together, lace your fingers, and rub your fingers up and down against each other.

6.
Cover a tight fist with a loose fist. Rub the backs of your fingers in the tight fist in the palm of the loose fist. Swap hands and repeat.

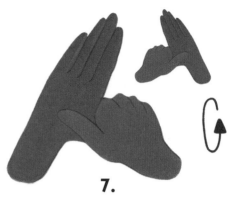

7.
Wrap a fist around the opposite hand's thumb and rub around it. Swap hands and repeat.

8.
Put one hand's fingertips together and rub them in a circle in the palm of the opposite hand. Swap hands and repeat.

9.
Rinse your hands with water until all the soap has washed off.

10.
Dry your hands with a clean towel.

Finishing all of these steps should take at least 20 seconds, which you can time by counting to 20 very slowly. To help you count slowly enough, you can say "bubble" in-between every number, for example: "One…bubble…two…bubble…three… bubble…" and so on to 20.

Good job, you're all clean! Now you can enjoy lunch with your family.

Mind Your Manners

When your family comes together for a meal, you might be expected to behave a certain way at the table. Polite behavior around the table is known as table manners. The rules people follow during mealtimes can be different depending on where they live in the world.

It is traditional in many East Asian countries to eat with chopsticks. These two smooth sticks are held in one hand, and used to bring food to your mouth. Stabbing food with your chopsticks or licking them is considered rude.

In Southern China, a typical meal consists of many platters of food that are put in the middle of the table. Each person also has an individual bowl of rice. Chopsticks are used to pick up bite-sized pieces of food from a platter and place them either into your bowl or your mouth. To eat rice, pick up your bowl, hold it very close to your mouth, and use your chopsticks to push the rice in. It's important to eat all the food you place in your bowl, but do not take the last bite of food from any of the shared platters. An adult may offer it to you, but it is impolite for a child to take the food on their own.

In many African countries it is traditional for people to eat with their hands. In Nigeria, it is polite to eat using only your right hand. Before eating, everyone washes their right hand in a little bowl of water, which is placed on the table. A popular dish is a spicy stew called *egusi* (eh-GOO-see). It is served with a dough called *fufu* (FOO-foo). To eat, you pull a small, bite-sized piece of *fufu* from the bigger piece on your plate. Roll it into a little ball and poke your thumb in the middle to make a tiny indent, then use it to scoop up a bite of stew. Into your mouth it goes!

In the South American country of Chile, you don't ever eat anything with your hands. A knife and fork are always used, even when eating sandwiches, pizza, or French fries.

In France, table manners involve keeping your wrists on the edge of the table instead of in your lap. As you eat, make sure you always have either a knife and fork, or a fork and a piece of bread, in your hands. And you must do your best to eat everything on your plate!

Table manners are not exactly the same everywhere in the world, or even in every family. But no matter what rules you follow, being polite during a meal shows the people you're with that you respect them, appreciate your food, and are happy to be spending time together.

Rules about table manners often change over time. But many are still the same as they were years ago. For example, in the United States a woman called Emily Post wrote a book about table manners back in 1922, and it was a huge success. Today, Post's family is responsible for keeping her rules of good manners up to date, and many people still follow them.

Here are a few of Emily Post's table manners for kids:

1. Make sure your hands and face are clean before coming to the table.
2. Chew with your mouth closed.
3. Ask for things to be passed to you instead of reaching.
4. Don't talk with food in your mouth.
5. Put your napkin on your lap.
6. Finish chewing before taking a drink.
7. Don't put your elbows on the table.
8. Ask whether you may be excused from the table when you are finished.

Are any of the children in this picture breaking Emily's rules? What would she suggest they do differently?

Cleaning Up

It's time to shake the house! Well, not exactly. But in Farsi, the most common language spoken in Iran, that's what the words for spring cleaning—*khāna tekānī* (KHAW-nuh te-KAW-NEE)—roughly mean. Iranian New Year begins on the first day of spring, which is usually around March 21. The celebration is called *Nowruz* (NO-rooz), which means "new day." It has been celebrated for more than 2,500 years. During *Nowruz*, families prepare to celebrate the new year by cleaning and tidying their homes from top to bottom. It's important to have a sparkly-clean house to welcome *Nowruz*.

Spring cleaning in the Jewish culture prepares families for Passover, which lasts for seven or eight days in either March or April. This holiday celebrates the ancient Hebrews' escape from slavery more than 3,000 years ago. During Passover, families avoid eating certain foods, called *chametz* (HA-mets). These include foods that use ingredients to make them rise, such as yeast in bread. Spring cleaning gets rid of every crumb of *chametz* from the house. Then it's time to celebrate!

Preparing for *Nowruz*

In Chinese culture, families begin to prepare for Chinese New Year during a special day called *Xiaonian* (tsiow-NI-an), which means "Little New Year." It usually falls during January or February, before the New Moon. On *Xiaonian,* everyone starts getting ready for the holiday by thoroughly cleaning and tidying their homes. By doing so, families hope to get rid of bad luck from the previous year, and to welcome a new year filled with good luck and joy. Happy Chinese New Year!

Preparing for Passover

Preparing for *Xiaonian*

There have probably been times when you were told to "clean your room!" And it might have seemed impossible if there was a big mess. But it can be easier than you think. Japanese organizing expert Marie Kondo has many tips on the subject. One of her methods for cleaning is to start by sorting items into categories. Here's how you can do it.

Pile up all the clothes that aren't where they belong. Sort them into two piles: clothes to hang in the closet or fold and put into drawers, and dirty clothes for the laundry. Put them all in their correct places. Great! Now on to the next items: books.

Gather all the books that belong on your bookshelf. When they're all together, arrange them neatly on the shelf. Maybe you sort them by the main color on the cover. Maybe you do it by size: tallest to shortest. Or maybe you do it another way. It's all up to you.

Now it's time to tackle the toys! Figure out which type of toy you want to put away first. Maybe it's all the blocks. In this case, find them all and put them in their correct place. What's next? Balls? Dolls? Stuffed animals? Collect everything from each category and put them where they belong.

Your room is probably looking neat and clean by now. Well done!

Often, part of cleaning up is getting rid of things you don't need anymore. One way to do this is to donate toys, clothes, or books to organizations that sell them to make money for charity or give them to people in need. Some people have donated so many unwanted things that they have set world records!

A group of people in the United Kingdom collected more than 7,500 plush toys for donation. Those stuffed animals surely brightened the day of all the children who received one to hug.

The most toys donated in one hour was 5,019, in New Orleans, Louisiana, in 2018. That's about 84 toys a minute!

The largest collection of donated clothes was made up of 565,798 items. Wow, that must have dressed a lot of people! The record was set in Saudi Arabia in May 2019.

In India, a group of people collected the largest single donation of school supplies. It weighed more than 39,709 pounds (18,012 kilograms). That's about the weight of three large, adult male Asian elephants!

Even if you don't have a record-breaking number of toys or clothes to donate, giving a few things that you no longer need may brighten up someone else's day. And knowing that you've helped others will probably make you feel good, too.

Storytime

Reading stories can be lots of fun. You can read on your own, or you can share stories with friends and family. Stories, like this one, are often written down in books. Some also have photographs or artworks to go along with the words. But did you know that some stories are never written down? They can be told aloud from memory or through paintings, drawings, music, or dance. Some stories are even sewn onto fabric.

Long ago, early humans painted pictures on the walls of caves. The oldest cave art ever found is in Indonesia. These paintings were made about 44,000 years ago and tell a story of humans hunting animals. People have continued to tell stories in paintings ever since.

Prehistoric people used charcoal, mud, and ground-up rocks and minerals to make paints.

Paintings that tell stories are called 'narrative art,' and many of them are on display in museums for people to enjoy. Visitors can look at each painting and think about the stories the artists were trying to tell.

Can you "read" the story in the painting below? Look at the art and describe what you see.

Some families share stories aloud, from memory. In western Africa, storytellers called griots (GRE-ohs) tell stories about their village's history, families, and traditions. These stories are either sung or spoken. Older griots teach younger ones all the information they know, so the stories are passed on and are never forgotten. Young griots may start memorizing stories when they are only eight years old. By the time they are about 18, they will have learned hundreds of songs and stories. As younger griots are learning, they also memorize people's birthdays, wedding dates, and when people died. A griot often sings a story while playing music on an instrument. Can you tell any stories from memory?

These griots are playing an instrument called a kora.

In Hawaii, the art of 'hula' tells stories through a combination of dancing, chanting, and singing. These stories are called *mo'olelo* (mo-oh-LEH-low). The movements used in hula dancing copy the gentle waves of the ocean. Dancers move their hips back and forth, and move their arms and hands gracefully in time with the chanting and music. Many of the *mo'olelo* are stories about the islands that make up Hawaii, and the people who live there. Young hula performers learn from the older dancers as a way of keeping the art alive through the generations.

Another way to tell stories is through fabric, such as quilts and tapestries. A quilt is a covering for a bed. It's made by sewing many small pieces of fabric together, such as scraps of worn-out clothing. These pieces of clothing tell stories about the people who wore them. By looking at the pieces, you might remember a favorite old T-shirt, a tie that your grandfather wore, or the soft pajamas that one of your siblings wore when they were a baby. There are so many memories that can be shared from just one quilt.

When pictures are woven onto cloth, they create a kind of storytelling art called a tapestry. The Bayeux Tapestry is one of the most famous in the world. It hangs in a museum in France and was made more than 900 years ago, soon after a huge battle during a war in England. The tapestry tells the story of that battle, as well as showing how people lived at the time. It shows more than 600 people, hundreds of animals, and dozens of ships and castles. You could spend hours looking at all the pictures and thinking about the stories in this tapestry.

A section of the Bayeux Tapestry

Animals in the Family

Many different animals make great family pets—they can be excellent company and lots of fun to play with. But animals haven't always lived with people.

Wolves are the ancestors of all modern dogs. In the past, they all lived in the wild. However, over time, some wolves gradually came to rely on humans for food. It is thought that this process started between 14,000 and 29,000 years ago in Eurasia (the land that is now Europe and Asia). The wolves would follow groups of humans who were hunting and eat any meat that was left behind.

As humans and wolves became more comfortable with each other, wolves started helping the humans by warning them when danger was near. This is similar to a pet dog barking when someone comes to the door. Over thousands of years, these friendly wolves gradually developed into the dogs that we know today.

Pet cats evolved from the Near Eastern wildcat in a similar way to how dogs evolved from wolves. In ancient Egypt, wildcats began to gather where people were growing crops. They didn't want to eat the crops, but rather the mice and rats that nibbled on the grains. People started to welcome having the wildcats around. Modern cats are still very good at hunting mice.

Today, there are about 470 million pet dogs and 370 million pet cats around the world. Clearly, the relationship between humans and their furry friends has worked out well!

We know that dogs bark and cats meow in order to communicate, but did you know that they also use body language as well as sounds to tell us things? If you pay attention, you can learn what they're saying. Here are some pet signals to look out for:

A cat's purr can mean lots of different things. If you stroke a cat and it starts to purr, it usually means that the cat is happy and relaxed. But cats also purr as a way of soothing themselves when they are hurt or scared, in the same way a child might suck their thumb.

If a playful pup sticks its bottom high up in the air while leaning down low on its front legs, it is telling you that it wants to play. This position is called a play bow. The dog might bark and bounce around, too!

When a dog lies on its back or side, with its front paws relaxed, it's probably asking for a belly rub. It's also letting you know that it trusts you.

Next time you have a chance to watch a dog or cat, try to guess what they're telling you!

Some families have specially trained animals, called service animals, to help with certain jobs. They need to be calm, smart, and eager to learn, and are often dogs. These traits can be found in many different dog breeds, but they are particularly strong in German shepherds and golden retrievers. This makes them ideal breeds for the intense training needed to become service dogs.

A service dog might be trained to help guide someone who cannot see well. While the dog is working, no one but the person it's guiding is allowed to touch or talk to it. But when the dog is off duty, it's just like a member of the family.

Other service dogs are trained to help people who can't move around very well. These dogs can fetch things, turn lights on and off, and open doors for their owner.

Hearing assistance dogs help people who cannot hear.
These dogs can let people know if the doorbell rings, a
baby is crying, or a smoke alarm is going off. To do this,
the pooch nudges the person and leads them to the sound.

When someone is sick,
having an animal to cuddle can
make them feel better. If they
don't have a pet, they can call
on special therapy animals to
do this job. These animals can be
friendly dogs, cuddly cats, fluffy
rabbits, squeaking guinea pigs,
or even horses that can offer
a comforting nuzzle with their
nose. The only rule is that the
service animal always has to
be very well-behaved.

The Great Outdoors

Fresh air, warm sunshine, and the smell of grass—welcome to the great outdoors! It's a playground for sports, wild adventures, and maybe even a space to grow your own plants.

An outdoor space can be your backyard, balcony, or a local park. It can be a place to play games such as soccer, tag, hide-and-seek, or Frisbee. In China, children might play a game called Catch the Dragon's Tail. In this game, friends and family line up by holding onto each other's shoulders. The person at the front is the dragon's head and must catch the person at the end—the dragon's tail. In Ghana, children might play a game called *Pilolo* (PEE-low-low), which is a treasure hunt and a running race in one!

No matter what the weather is like where you live, there's usually a way to make the most of being outside. If it's wet, you can slip on some rain boots to splish-splash in puddles. If it's warm, you can have water fights, run through a sprinkler, or swim in a pool to cool down. If you live somewhere that it snows, you can build a snowman!

Carrots

Garlic

Zucchini

Tomatoes

Cauliflower

Radishes

Edible flowers

Beets

Gardens change throughout the seasons. In places like North America and Europe, flowers begin to grow in spring and bloom through the summer. In fall, leaves on the trees turn red, orange, or yellow before dropping to the ground. In some places, such as the South Asian country of Sri Lanka, the weather is always warm and there are periods of very heavy rains, called monsoons. In this type of climate, plants grow and flowers bloom all year long.

Flowers attract butterflies and bees.

A seedling pops out of the ground.

Plants start their lives as seeds, which come in many shapes and sizes. To grow a plant, place a seed in some soil, cover it up, and water it. When a tiny stem and leaves push up above the ground, the plant has begun to sprout. At this stage it is known as a seedling.

Just like animals, plants need food to grow. They make food using water, sunlight, and a gas called carbon dioxide, which is what humans breathe out. So, some people talk or sing to their plants to help them grow. In return, plants make oxygen, which is what humans breathe in.

Plants don't always need to be planted by people. Insects and animals can help plants grow, too. Squirrels are especially great at this. In the fall, they collect nuts, such as acorns, from trees, which they hide in the ground and dig up to eat in winter. Sometimes, the squirrels forget about their stash and the seeds are left to grow. Eventually, they will become tall trees, in which future squirrels might scramble and play.

Flowers need to be pollinated in order to make seeds. This is when pollen (a dusty substance made by plants) is transferred from one plant to another. Bees are great pollinators. When they land on a flower, pollen sticks to their hairs. Then, as they buzz from flower to flower, the pollen rubs off the bees onto the other flowers that they visit.

The outdoors is full of many awesome creatures. If you take a moment to stop and look up, you might see birds soaring through the sky. To encourage them to visit you, why not put a bird feeder outside your window or in your yard? Fill it with birdseed, and lots of feathered friends might stop by for a snack.

No matter where you live, there is always nature outside. If you look, you can enjoy the birds, bees, bugs, and everything else the natural world has to offer where you are. Better yet, ask a parent, sibling, or friend to join you, so you can share the experience together.

Fun at the Playground

Do you like going to the playground with your family and friends? Maybe you enjoy climbing on the jungle gym, swinging on the swings, or whooshing down the slide? *Wheee!*

Children have always liked to play outdoors. In fact, some scientists have even discovered ancient Greek pottery painted with scenes showing women and children on swings.

The first playgrounds were created in Germany in the 1800s. They were called "sand gardens," and were created by a teacher named Friedrich Froebel. The sand garden was a very simple sand box that gave children a safe place to play with one another and enjoy the outdoors.

One of the first playgrounds in the United States was opened in 1887. Over time, more playgrounds were built, and they became bigger and more popular. Playgrounds provided a space for kids to meet up with friends, run around, and play games. The USA now has more than 10,000 playgrounds across the country for children to enjoy.

Playgrounds are also places where you can see science in action. Many pieces of playground equipment use the force of gravity and different types of energy to work. Science can explain how it's possible to swing high into the air or spin round and round on the merry-go-round.

When swinging on your own, without someone pushing you, you lean back and stretch your legs out straight. This action uses energy from your body to move the swing forward. When it begins to swing backward, you quickly lean forward and pull your legs back, bending at the knees. This action helps move the swing backward. The harder you pump your legs, the higher you will swing.

Lean forward, legs tucked in!

Lean back,
legs out!

The speed that is created as you swing back and forth is called kinetic energy, which is the type of energy that creates movement. At the two highest points of the swinging motion, where your swing pauses before you change direction, you have potential energy. The swing turns the potential energy into kinetic energy, then back into potential energy. This continues over and over. The higher you swing, the more potential energy you gain. Turning one kind of energy into the other repeatedly is what allows you to fly through the air.

All playgrounds are different. Some might have swings and a slide, or maybe a jungle gym. Others might have splash pads or water zones to cool off in when it's hot. Some could have a train for you to ride, rope bridges to cross, or even trampolines to jump on!

Today, many playgrounds are designed to be accessible. This means they are designed so that kids of all abilities can enjoy them. These playgrounds might have extra features, such as a ramp that makes it easier for wheelchair users to reach the top of a slide. Once at the top, you can slide down to the cushioned landing spot below. There might also be a merry-go-round designed without a step up, and with areas wide enough for a wheelchair to fit in. This means you can roll right on, ready to spin around and around. Don't get too dizzy!

If you could design your dream playground, what would it include? Would it have an ocean theme with giant ships to sail? Or maybe a jungle theme with monkey bars and rope bridges? Maybe you would enjoy a zip line to whoosh from one side of the playground to the other? The possibilities are endless!

Camping Adventures

In 1853, a British family of two parents and eight children traveled to the United States. The Holding family was hoping to make a new life there and spent five weeks camping on the Mississippi River. Then, they waited to join a wagon train—a group of families traveling in covered wagons pulled by horses. The wagon train would take them across the country, from east to west. Nine-year-old Thomas Hiram Holding loved this adventure. Little did he know that it was just the beginning of his lifelong love of the great outdoors.

Thomas never forgot how much he enjoyed camping as a child. As a young adult, he camped every chance he got. But camping equipment in those days was large, heavy, and hard to move around. Thomas longed for a way to go further into the wilderness. So, he began inventing camping equipment that was easier to move around.

He figured out how to make a simple, lightweight tent of canvas and ropes. Then, he tried carrying his supplies around on a bicycle, which was a new invention at the time. Thomas went on to invent a lightweight stove and other useful equipment. He even wrote a book called *The Camper's Handbook*, which was full of camping advice. Thomas eventually became known as the "Father of Modern-day Camping."

Today, families can travel far and wide on camping adventures, because any heavy equipment can be carried in a car. If you'd rather be closer to home, you can simply set up camp in your backyard!

If you're new to camping, there are a few simple essentials that you will need. First, a tent. A tent can be small, just for one person, or large enough for ten or more people. This is great if you have a big family. Each camper needs a sleeping bag and, for extra comfort, a cushioned mat to put underneath.

It's important to bring food to eat as well as a lantern or flashlight for nighttime. It's also a good idea to bring some camping chairs so everyone can sit comfortably. If there are logs or tree stumps nearby, you could use those as seats, too.

Before bedtime, campers sometimes gather around the campfire. You can roast marshmallows, drink hot chocolate, and tell stories. But don't forget to put the fire out before you go to sleep.

If you don't like the idea of sleeping in a tent, then a recreational vehicle (RV) would be perfect for you. They are a great way of bringing the comforts of home with you as you go on your outdoor adventure. RVs can be driven wherever you'd like to go, and they provide places to sleep, eat, use the bathroom, and relax.

Here are some of the things you might find in an RV.

In the kitchen, you might have a fridge, stove, and counter.

A double bed sits over the cab. Sometimes there is even a window through which you can see the night sky.

A sheet of canvas, called an awning, unfolds outside, creating a nice shady spot to sit.

As your family drives to your camping spot, each of you has a comfortable seat, and everything you've packed is safely stored away for the drive. Once you're at the campsite, the set-up begins to create your home away from home.

The bathroom usually comes complete with a toilet, shower, and sink.

Some RVs have solar panels on the roof. They generate energy, which can be used to power the lights and appliances.

Seats in the living room area can also convert into a bed.

Sometimes there's a bike rack on the back of the RV. With your bikes handy, you'll be ready to go exploring at a moment's notice!

Splashing Around

Are you learning to swim? If so, you're in good company. In fact, some researchers think that people may have started to swim way back in the Stone Age, up to 10,000 years ago. In an area of the Sahara in southwest Egypt, there is a cave called the Cave of Swimmers. Pictures of Stone Age humans decorate its walls. They appear to be splashing, diving, and swimming playfully.

"I am using the breaststroke."

There are a few different types of swimming moves that you can use in the water. These moves are called swimming strokes. One is the breaststroke. When doing the breaststroke, you push your arms out from your chest and sweep them around to your side. Then, you kick your legs out and around behind you, just like a frog.

"I prefer using the backstroke."

"I like using the butterfly."

For a different view while you swim, you can do the backstroke. In this stroke, you stretch out on your back and move forward by kicking your feet. Your arms swing backward over your head one at a time.

Then there's the butterfly, one of the fastest swimming strokes. It is also one of the hardest to master. You need to swim straight on your stomach while moving your legs up and down in a wave-like motion, similar to a mermaid. Your arms sweep forward up and over your head at the same time, making the shape of butterfly wings. As your arms swing down through the water, your body is pushed upward so that you can take a breath above the surface. Have you tried any of these strokes? Or perhaps a different one?

Learning to swim is important. It keeps you safe in the water. But swimming is also about having a good time. There are all sorts of swimming toys and floating aids, such as rubber rings, armbands, and colorful noodles that help keep you above the water. In medieval times, however, Japanese samurai warriors gave themselves a swimming challenge. They trained to swim in their heavy, metal armor! Some schools of martial arts trained this way into the 21st century and practiced in the local swimming pool.

Swimming pools are some of the best places to have fun in the water. And there are many different types. Some are built with slides, waterfalls, diving boards, fountains, or even wave machines. In Las Vegas there is a pool called "The Tank." Why does it have this name? The pool surrounds a shark tank! Here, you can swim side by side with sharks, protected by a see-through wall. For an extra thrill, zoom down the three-story water slide that runs through a tube in the middle of the tank!

Swimming pools aren't the only places to swim. If you've ever swum in the ocean, a lake, a pond, a river, or a stream, you've been wild swimming. Someone who really took wild swimming to the extreme is Martin Strel, a man from the European country of Slovenia. He swam more than 3,107 miles (5,000 kilometers) in the Amazon River in South America. Strel holds the Guinness World Record for the longest swim—it took him 67 days! But he wasn't alone. The mighty Amazon River is home to pink river dolphins, manatees, electric eels, colorful fish, snakes, and even alligator-like creatures called caiman.

You don't need to travel to one of the world's longest rivers to meet a variety of water-dwelling animals. You can simply visit your nearest lake, stream, beach, or seaside tide pool. Look carefully and you can find sea urchins, seagulls, or even seaweed. If you plan to explore any kind of watery place, make sure an adult is with you. And while you're exploring, see if you can impress them with the number of creatures you can count!

The Wonder of Trees

From hiking and playing games to just sitting outside and soaking up the sunshine, there are countless ways to enjoy being outside as a family. Depending on where you live, the world around you will look, feel, and smell very different. However, something that most of us can spot no matter where we live is trees.

There are more than 60,000 species of trees on Earth and they come in all shapes and sizes. In the UK, you might find forests of tall, thin silver birch trees. These trees have silvery-white bark that peels off from their trunks like sheets of paper.

In Australia, where the weather is much warmer, eucalyptus trees are very common. Koalas love to sit on the branches and munch the leaves.

On the island of Madagascar, you'll see many towering baobab trees. These trees have very thick trunks and thin, root-like branches. Baobab trees are very special because they can provide food, water, and shelter to the animals and people who live nearby. Hollowed-out baobab trees are used to store rainwater for people to drink during the dry season. Each tree is looked after by a family who monitors how much water is inside.

Spending time among the trees can be very good for you. In Japan, many people take part in *shinrin-yoku* (shin-rin yo-koo) or "forest bathing," which is the practice of being calm and feeling at peace among trees. When you are forest bathing, you try to focus on the natural world around you and soak up its beauty, just like you might soak in a bath.

Next time you are out and about with your family, why not give forest bathing a try? While you're out among the trees, leave any technology at home or in your backpack so you're not interrupted. Then, walk around slowly. Notice the ground under your feet. Listen for the crunch of fallen leaves, or on a rainy day, feel the squishy earth sink a little as you walk. Take deep breaths through your nose to help slow your heart rate and calm your body. At the same time, notice the smell of the trees. Then stop moving—stay very still and quiet. Look, listen, feel, and smell everything that is around you.

When you've finished forest bathing, take a moment to think about how you feel. Are you relaxed? Do you feel happy and energized?

Some trees are truly awesome, and even record-breaking. The tallest tree is a coast redwood called Hyperion, which grows in California. When it was last measured, the tree was almost 380 feet (116 meters) tall. That's taller than the Statue of Liberty!

The world's thickest tree is a Montezuma cypress located in Mexico. It is about 38 feet (12 meters) wide. You could fit a double-decker bus inside its trunk! The oldest tree ever recorded in the world is a Great Basin bristlecone pine in California called Methuselah. It is more than 4,850 years old!

Next time you see a tree, stop for a moment to take a look at it. Notice the shape of its leaves and the feel of its bark. Think about the many families who could have walked by it or sat under it for shade on a hot, sunny day. Maybe there are animal families that have made their homes in it, too.

Pedal Power

Ding, ding, ding! Make way, bicycles coming through! Family bike rides can be lots of fun. Just clip on your helmet, jump on the saddle, and off you go.

Bicycles allow you to zoom around with little effort. You can travel much faster on a bike than you can by walking or running. Traditional bicycles have two wheels that you turn by pushing pedals with your feet. The pedals are connected to the wheels by a chain, and the faster you pedal, the faster the bike goes.

To stop your bike, just use the brakes by squeezing the brake levers on the handlebars. When you do this, the brake pads will clamp down on the rear wheels. This brings you safely to a standstill.

Saddle

Brake

Chain

Peda

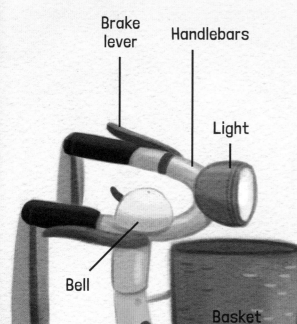

Brake lever

Handlebars

Light

Bell

Basket

Wheel

Tire

Some bicycles have gears, which help you go faster and make it much easier to cycle up and down hills. Gears are a system of cogs that control how many times the wheels turn for each push of the pedals.

The wheels of a bike are probably the most important part. A bicycle without wheels wouldn't go very far! Bicycle wheels have tires filled with air that make your ride more comfortable and help to grip the surface of the ground. This stops your bike from slipping if you're riding in the rain.

The first bicycle-like machine, called a *draisienne* (dray-zee-EN), was invented in Germany more than 200 years ago. It had no pedals, so the rider pushed themselves along with their feet on the ground. Bikes have come a long way since then. Now there are lots of different types to choose from.

Racing bikes allow the rider to go super-fast. They have narrow, tall wheels and thin, lightweight frames.

BMX bikes are built for doing tricks. They have much smaller frames than other bikes, so that the rider can lift or swing the bike around while riding.

Mountain bikes have thick, bumpy tires that grip the dirt when a person cycles up and down hilly or bumpy trails. Riders often wear special glasses and helmets to protect their faces from mud, rain, or bugs when they ride in the woods.

Handcycles are great for people who aren't able to use their legs well. These bicycles can be pedaled by hand and often have three wheels to keep the bike stable.

Tandem bicycles are made for two, three, or more people to ride together. They have multiple seats and handlebars all fixed to two wheels.

A balance bike is perfect for kids who are learning to ride. They look just like traditional bicycles, but with no pedals, similar to the *draisienne*. The rider pushes themselves along and brakes by putting their feet on the ground.

Unlike most cars, which have engines that pollute the air, bicycles are powered by their riders. They are clean, green riding machines. To reduce car traffic, many cities have made it easier and safer for people to ride bicycles instead.

One of these cities is Amsterdam in the Netherlands. In this city there are hundreds of bike lanes, making it one of the most bicycle-friendly places in the world. The people of Amsterdam love their bicycles. In fact, there are more bicycles than people! You'll often see whole families riding together to school, to visit friends, to go shopping, or just for fun.

The great thing about riding a bicycle is that once you learn, you'll never forget how to do it. That's where the phrase "It's just like riding a bicycle" comes from—it refers to something you've learned that you will never forget.

How many bicycles
can you count in
this picture?

Let's Go Shopping!

Do you know where your food comes from? Early humans got their food by hunting, fishing, and gathering fruit, nuts, and other plant parts. Then, about 10,000 years ago, people began to grow their own food and became farmers. At first, most families lived and worked on farms. Today, in many parts of the world, a few farms grow the food for everyone.

If you don't live on a farm, how do you get food? You could visit a farmer's market where all the food is brought in from local farms.

In Barcelona, Spain, there is an outdoor market called La Boqueria. It was opened in the 1200s and is still there today. Your family can find lots of tasty food there, such as fish, meat, cheese, vegetables, and fruit. You can walk from stall to stall, picking out the food you want to buy, and paying the person selling it.

In Quito, Ecuador, your family might shop at the big Mercado Central, or central market. You can choose from many different kinds of bananas and more than ten kinds of potatoes. But those are just the most popular varieties. There are actually 300 kinds of bananas and up to 500 kinds of potatoes that grow in Ecuador's warm, rainy climate.

Many people around the world shop in grocery stores. At a grocery store, your family walks through the aisles picking out the food that you want and putting it into a basket or a shopping cart. Some supermarkets have special counters where you can find meat, fish, baked goods, cheese, and prepared food, such as pizza. People working behind the counter package up the things you ask for. Then you can add them to your basket or cart.

It takes a lot of workers to keep a grocery store running smoothly. One important job is restocking the shelves so that customers can always find what they're looking for. Truck drivers deliver the food from farms, ranches, and factories where packaged foods are made. A grocery store also has cleaners to keep the store spick-and-span. Managers supervise the store to make sure everyone does their job properly.

Once you have everything you want, you take it to the checkout counter. A cashier will use a computer to scan the barcodes on the packages. The barcodes are little black-and-white striped images that tell the computer how much an item costs. Once the cashier has scanned everything, you can pay for your groceries and take it all home to cook a delicious meal.

Of course shopping isn't just about buying food. There are lots of other things families need, too. Some are big items, such as cars. Others are smaller things, such as pens and pencils. Sometimes, we might even get to go toy shopping. A trip to the toy store with your family is often exciting, whether you're there to buy a gift for someone else or a toy for yourself.

If you and your family were to shop at LARK Toys, in Kellogg, Minnesota, you could take a turn on the carousel. You can choose to ride on any of the colorful, hand-carved animals. There is a dragon, a flamingo, a wolf, and even a chicken to ride on. After your ride, you can head over to meet a real animal—the store is home to a few pet miniature llamas!

The Hakuhinkan Toy Park is a toy store in Tokyo, Japan. It has a big racetrack set up inside where you can race slot cars with other children. These little vehicles zoom along in slots, or grooves, along a track.

Hamleys, a toy store in London, UK, is considered the largest and oldest in the world. It'll take you and your family hours to explore all seven floors!

Up, Down, Round and Round

Zip, spin, swing, twist, turn, plunge, and swoosh! Are you ready for a trip to the theme park? Many families love going to theme parks. They have exciting rides, interesting shows and performances, and even treats to eat. Modern theme parks might even have a farm, a model village, or a water park.

Bakken pleasure garden in the 1930s

In medieval times, people in Europe visited amusement parks, called pleasure gardens, for fun. In Denmark, the Bakken pleasure garden is still operating. This park opened in 1583 after natural water springs were discovered there. Entertainers began to perform for the people who came to visit the springs, and the amusement park started to grow. It now has about 150 attractions, and people can still ride on a wooden roller coaster that was built in 1932.

By the late 1800s, amusement parks began using new technologies. At Coney Island in New York, there was a giant Ferris wheel, a go-kart track, and a ride called the Steeplechase, where people could ride along a track on wooden "galloping" horses.

Today's theme parks have even more exciting rides. There are giant pendulums that swing people back and forth, bungee rides that fling people up into the air, gigantic Ferris wheels, and speedy roller coasters, to name just a few. These rides have been built to keep the riders safe, even while turned upside down in the air. But why don't you fall out of an upside-down roller coaster?

The laws of physics can help explain. Physics is the science of energy and the different forces that affect how things move. Roller coasters use a couple of different forces: one is called gravity and the other is called inertia. Roller coaster cars are usually pulled up to the top of a large hill by a strong cable. Then, the cars are pulled down the hill by the force of gravity, which is what draws everything on Earth toward the ground.

As the cars shoot down the track, they build up speed. By the time the cars reach a loop or a section where they turn upside down, they are traveling very fast. At such a fast speed, inertia pulls the passengers into their seats. This means that they can be tipped this way, that way, and upside down, but still stay safely in the car. *Wheeee!* Riders are also buckled into their seats with tight straps.

Some theme parks around the world are home to record-breaking rides, and many are perfect for thrill-seeking families.

The fastest roller coaster in the world is at Ferrari World, in the city of Abu Dhabi in the United Arab Emirates. The ride is designed like an Italian racetrack. It thrusts you forward at 149 miles per hour (240 kilometers per hour) in just under five seconds. It's so fast that the riders at the front have to wear goggles.

In a theme park called Escape, in the Asian country of Malaysia, visitors will find the world's longest water slide. A trip down this slide lasts for an incredible three minutes and takes people whizzing through the surrounding forest.

The Twistosaurus at Flamingo Land in North Yorkshire, UK, is famous for a different reason. It might not be the biggest or fastest ride, but it's where a man named Jack Reynolds set the record for being the oldest person to ride on a roller coaster. He was 105! Jack rode the Twistosaurus with his daughter, Jayne, in order to raise money for a local charity. You can never be too old for a family fun day!

It's Vacation Time

Let's go away on an adventure! Would you like to build sandcastles on a warm, sunny beach? Or perhaps you'd like to visit the snowy mountains or a lake? The world is full of exciting places to explore.

Earth is shaped like a soccer ball, and has an imaginary line, called the equator, that runs around its center. Near the equator it's very hot. In general, the farther from the equator you travel, the colder it becomes. When planning a vacation, it's useful to think about how hot or cold your destination will be. To work this out, look at a map to see where your vacation spot is, in relation to the equator. You can also find out what season it will be when you visit. Places that are farther away from the equator usually have changing seasons. In these places, the weather will be warmer in summer and colder in the winter.

Some countries have mountains, some have deserts, some have rain forests, and some have a mix of landscapes. There's no shortage of things to see no matter where you go on your vacation, even if you don't go far from home.

Where will your travels take you?

Equator

97

Once your trip has been planned, the packing begins. You will have to think carefully about what you'd like to take with you because it will all need to fit in your suitcase. If your family is traveling to Norway in January, for example, it will be very cold. Everyone will need to pack plenty of warm clothes. What else would you pack to visit a cold place? Warm socks would be perfect. So would a fluffy hat, gloves, a jacket, thermal layers, a scarf, and maybe even snow boots.

How about a vacation near the sea—maybe to the Spanish coast in August? The contents of this suitcase will look entirely different. Let's put in a sun hat, swimming gear, shorts, T-shirts, sunglasses, plenty of sunscreen, and, if there's room, a bucket and shovel.

If wildlife adventuring in South Africa or Brazil is what you prefer, it would be useful to take some extra-special gear. Binoculars for bird watching and bug spray to keep mosquitoes away would be very handy.

Wherever you go, you'll need to pack the essentials.
Don't forget a toothbrush, underwear, and pajamas.
You may also want to bring along your favorite toy
and your favorite book to keep you company.

For vacations to countries where people speak a different language from yours, it's helpful to prepare a few words to say. How about learning the word for "hello?" Here is how you say it in a few different languages:

1. French: *bonjour* (bon-ZHOOR)
2. German: *hallo* (HA-low)
3. Spanish: *hola* (OH-lah)
4. Arabic: *marhaba* (MAR-ha-ba)
5. Japanese: *konnichiwa* (kon-nee-chee-wah)

Happy Birthday to You!

A birthday is a celebration of the day you were born. Families around the world celebrate birthdays in many different ways. One way is by preparing and eating special foods.

Can you guess where you'd eat fairy bread on your birthday? In Australia and New Zealand! To make this special treat, you spread white bread with butter and cut it into little triangles. Then, cover it with little sugar sprinkles called "hundreds and thousands." It's colorful *and* delicious!

In South Korea, many people eat a soup called *miyeok-guk* (mie-YUCK-guck) on their birthdays. It is made with seaweed and served on this special day as a way of honoring mothers. This is because many Korean women eat this soup right after having their babies. It is full of nutritious ingredients that help them recover from giving birth.

If it's your birthday in Russia, you're given a fruit pie that has a birthday greeting carved into the pastry on top. The pie in this picture says "Happy birthday!"

In Holland, the ages 5, 10, 15, 20, and 21 are known as your "crown years." On these special birthdays, you usually have a fruit tart for breakfast, but pancakes are also popular.

Birthday parties offer a great opportunity for families and friends to come together and celebrate. A fun game played at birthday parties In Mexico is hitting a piñata (pee-nyah-tah). A piñata is made with layers of paper and glue shaped into a colorful, hollow figure. Candy is hidden inside. If it's your birthday, you get the first turn at the game. This is how it works: you hit the piñata with a stick to try to break it so all the candy falls out. But there's a twist. You have to do it blindfolded! Everyone takes turns until the piñata breaks apart. Then it's a free-for-all as everyone scrambles to collect some candy!

When a baby is born, it enters its first year of life. In China, it is common to say that a newborn baby is "one," because it is in its first year. When the baby has its first birthday, it is now "two" because it is starting its second year. At this point, many Chinese people have a celebration called the *zhua zhou* (chua-choe), which means the "birthday grab." Your parents surround you with a collection of different toys. These might include a toy airplane, a musical instrument, a stethoscope, a camera, a pen, or a calculator. Whichever toy you grab first is meant to tell your family, in a playful way, what you'll be when you grow up. For example, if you choose the camera first, maybe you'll become a photographer. What toy would match what you want to be when you grow up?

Putting candles on a cake is a common way to celebrate birthdays around the world. You can make a wish as you blow out the candles. Some people believe that if you blow out all the candles with one breath, your wish will come true.

It is thought that this tradition dates back to the ancient Greeks. They made round cakes in the shape of the Moon, to honor Artemis, the goddess of the Moon. They lit candles to remind them of moonlight. The smoke from the blown-out candles was believed to carry prayers and wishes up to the gods.

Here's a cool way to think about how old you are. No matter where on Earth you live, or how you celebrate being a year older, it always takes Earth one year to orbit, or travel around, the Sun. You are on Earth, of course, so you're along for the ride! How many times have you traveled around the Sun?

In case you'd like to wish someone a happy birthday in a different language, here are some options for you to try:

1. Spanish: *¡Feliz cumpleaños!* (feh-LEES koom-pleh-AH-nyohs)
2. French: *Bon anniversaire!* (bon ah-ni-ver-SERE)
3. Vietnamese: *Chúc mừng sinh nhật* (cheuk-mung-sing-nyat)
4. Swahili: *Furaha ya kuzaliwa* (foo-RAH-ha ya koo-zah-LEE-wah)
5. Welsh: *Penblwydd hapus* (PEN-blue-ith HA-pis)

Growing Families

All families are different. When a new baby is born, a family might grow bigger by one (or maybe two if twins are born!).

There are lots of ways to welcome a new baby into the world. Some welcoming ceremonies are religious, others are not, but they all celebrate the happy arrival of a newborn.

When a baby is born in the Netherlands, "cookies with mice" are served to guests to celebrate the birth. Thankfully, the "mice" in this tradition are actually seeds coated in sugar that are placed on the cookies.

In Bali, babies are thought to be very holy and are treated with great care and respect. For the first 105 days of their life, a newborn baby's feet are not allowed to touch the ground.

In Nigeria, a grandmother (or another close relative or friend) is the first to bathe a newborn. This is their way of welcoming the baby into the family. Can you think of ways that you might welcome a new baby?

Every person in the world was once a baby—including you! As a baby grows, lots of amazing things happen. Not only do babies grow bigger, but they start to understand and interact with the world around them, too.

Newborn babies need to be fed regularly and can only drink their mother's milk or formula for the first six months of their lives. A one-day-old's stomach is roughly the size of a marble. However, after just one week, their stomach is already the size of an apricot!

Babies grow really fast. Most will grow roughly 3/4 inch (2 centimeters) per month, which is about half as tall as a LEGO figure. Thankfully, this growth rate slows down as they get older. If babies kept growing at this speed, by the time they were adults they would be taller than a house!

Some scientists think that babies can recognize voices before they are even born. It is important to talk or sing to babies so that they learn to recognize words. And eventually they will begin to talk to you, too.

Families grow in lots of ways. Sometimes a new baby is born into the family. Or they might join the family through adoption. When grown-ups who already have children get married, their two families might join together as one. This is called a blended family. When this happens, there can be many new siblings at the same time, as well as new parents, grandparents, aunts, uncles, cousins, and more!

As we grow older, we might form close bonds with our friends. They can be our family, too. No matter how a group of people become a family, it's great to know that you can always be there for each other. Family members are great when you need a hug, a laugh, or someone to play with.

Getting Married

Have you ever been to a wedding? When two people get married, the event will often bring family and friends together for a joyful celebration. There are many different kinds of marriage ceremonies, celebrations, and traditions around the world. Some wedding ceremonies take place in a church, synagogue, temple, or other place of worship. Others might be held in a park, on a beach, or in a garden.

At a wedding there might be a ceremony in which the couple shares vows, which are the promises that they make to one another. Afterward there might be a party, or reception, with food, music, and dancing.

India is a big country with many different wedding traditions. One marriage custom is that the couple both wear red, which is thought to be a lucky color. At some Indian weddings, the groom arrives on an elephant, a white horse, or in a fancy car. At the end of the wedding the bride is carried on a sedan chair—a seat on a platform held up on the shoulders of friends and family members. In the past, the bride was traditionally carried all the way to her groom's house.

In Japan, some people follow a religion called Shinto. During a traditional Shinto wedding ceremony, the couple drink sake, a Japanese alcoholic drink. Each person takes three sips, three times, from three different cups. Sometimes the couple's parents will take sips, too. The ceremony is meant to signify the bond between the two families.

In Australia, wedding guests bring small stones to the ceremony. Everyone then places their stones all together in a bowl. The newlyweds take home the gift, called the unity bowl, to remind them of all the people who love and support them.

In Germany, as soon as a couple gets married, they saw a log in half in front of all their guests. Why? If they manage to saw it all the way through, the couple proves that they can work well together, as they'll need to do in their marriage.

Mandarin ducks and geese pair for life. This is why they are symbols of love and faithfulness in Korea. It used to be tradition for a Korean man to give live ducks and geese to the family of the woman he wanted to marry. Today, wooden carvings of a pair of ducks or geese are often given as wedding gifts instead.

During some wedding receptions in the Philippines, the happy couple releases two white doves. These birds are symbols of peace and harmony, which the newlyweds hope for in their marriage.

A playful tradition at Peruvian wedding receptions is called the cake pull. Several ribbons are placed underneath the wedding cake. Just one of the ribbons has a ring tied to it. Guests at the celebration are invited to pull a ribbon from the cake, and the one who gets the ring is said to be next to get married.

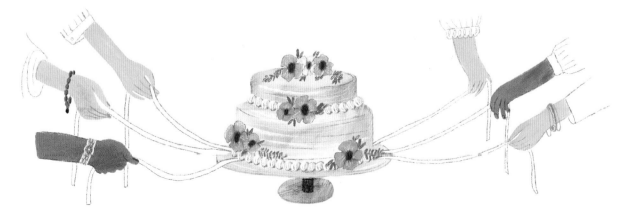

Other couples prefer more unusual types of weddings. Some choose to get married as they parachute out of an airplane or while they're scuba diving. People have also been married on a glacier, deep underground in a cave, or high up on Mount Everest. Couples have even been married while zooming up and down on a roller coaster!

Wheee!

Woohoo!

Saying Farewell

When someone's life comes to an end, it is usually a time when family and friends come together. They show love for each other and for the person who has gone. Sometimes, there is a ceremony called a funeral. Humans have held different types of funerals since ancient times.

In the Philippines, people practice various funeral traditions. In Cavite, a province on the island of Luzon, the Caviteño people are laid to rest inside trees. When a person has died, their friends and family hollow out the inside of a tree trunk and place the body carefully inside. The Caviteño people see this as giving back to the trees that provide them food and firewood while they are alive.

The Igbo people of southern Nigeria in Africa have a funeral tradition called *ikwa ozu* (IK-wa OH-zoo), which means "celebrating the dead." They believe that when someone dies, it is not the end, but rather the beginning of that person's journey to another world. This is an occasion for a large ceremony with food, drink, and dancing, which can last for days.

In many cultures, being buried with valuables is an important tradition. During ancient times, it was common for burial sites to be filled with gold, ceramic bowls, statues, and precious stones. It was often thought that the person who had passed away would take the items with them to another world or new life.

Chinese Emperor Qin Shi Huang was buried with an army of more than 8,000 clay soldiers and horses, called the Terracotta Army. The statues were built to real size and were made to protect the Emperor after his death. These impressive sculptures were positioned standing in rows, like real soldiers would. The burial chamber was discovered in 1974 by some farmers as they dug a well near the Chinese city of Xi'an. The army had been buried for around 2,000 years.

Vikings, the ancient people of Northern Europe, often cremated, or burned, their dead. But the very wealthy were given a different kind of funeral. They were buried in their ships, surrounded by weapons, such as spears and shields, as well as jewelry and their animals. In Oseberg, Norway, a huge burial ship that was more than 1,000 years old was found with the skeletons of two women inside. It is thought that one of the women could have been a famous Norse queen named Queen Asa. Boat burials happened in many cultures where sailing was important, including the Dong Son culture of Vietnam and the Anglo-Saxons of England.

When funerals and rituals are over, there is often time to remember those who have left us. Different families have their own ways of remembering the people they love. They may go to a cemetery and lay flowers on a grave, where a person's body is buried. They might light some incense at a temple or an altar and sit quietly to think about their family member or friend. Or they might gather together with others to talk and share stories.

Cemeteries are peaceful places to remember the dead. They can also be unexpectedly full of life. Some have grown wild and beautiful with plants and animals. The Green-Wood Cemetery in Brooklyn, New York, is home to more than 7,500 trees. Such a wealth of plants attracts a great variety of insects. A brand-new species of jewel beetle was even discovered in a beech tree in the Green-Wood Cemetery.

The Malagasy people of Madagascar, Africa, have a different way of remembering. Every few years after someone has died, their friends and relatives will visit their tomb. A tomb is a building or structure in which a person is laid to rest. The person is wrapped in new burial cloths in a ritual called *Famadihana* (fa-mah-DEE-hana) or "the turning of the bones." Families honor their ancestors by giving them care and attention, and also use this special time to share news about their lives with one another.

No matter how different cultures and different people remember loved ones, it is a personal choice. Everyone finds the path that is right for them.

Let's Celebrate!

A festival is a big celebration that brings together families, neighbors, friends, and visitors for one huge party. A festival can celebrate lots of different things, such as peoples' cultures and traditions, nature and harvests, certain times in a country's history, or love and understanding.

Festivals are also a way of keeping families connected to their cultural history. Many festivals started as a way of passing along stories from adults to children so that culture and traditions wouldn't be forgotten.

Chinese New Year is a 15-day festival that is celebrated in China and in Chinese communities around the world. It begins with the New Moon that happens sometime between January 21 and February 20. As well as cleaning their homes, people also welcome in the new year by having special meals and wearing the lucky color red. The Lantern Festival takes place on the last day. It includes a parade with a dragon dance. The dragon is the Chinese symbol of good fortune.

The Holi festival, or the "Festival of Colors," takes place every year around March. It is a religious festival for people of the Hindu faith. Holi celebrates good winning over evil. It also marks the end of winter and the beginning of spring, one of the three Indian harvest seasons. It's a holiday for repairing and starting new relationships, too.

For many people, Holi is a time for fun. At this outdoor festival, people throw brightly colored powder and water on one another. Streets turn into rainbows of color, and so does everyone taking part. Different colors symbolize different things. For example, red can symbolize love and green can stand for a fresh start.

Mexicans celebrate *Día de los Muertos* each year in November to honor their loved ones who have died. The name means "Day of the Dead." It's a happy time, meant for remembering good things about people who are gone. During the festival, families clean up graves and create altars with candles, flowers, decorated sugar skulls, and even the loved one's favorite foods. People might also dress up in special clothes and paint their faces

Carnival is a festival that is celebrated in many countries in February or March, right before a 40-day religious time known as Lent. During Lent, Christians traditionally give up certain foods and luxuries. Carnival began as a food festival. It was a time when people could eat the foods that they would soon be giving up for Lent. Now, Carnival is about more than food—it's a big party with dancing, music, parades, and costumes.

In Brazil, Carnival celebrations are big and colorful and include samba, a style of dancing and drumming. Many children go to samba schools and practice all year. They hope to perform during one of Carnival's spectacular parades, such as those held in the seaside city of Rio de Janeiro. Families line the streets to watch and cheer as the samba dancers and other performers march past.

Does your family participate in any festivals? If you could make up your own festival, what would you like to celebrate?

Family Reunions

Gather up your family members from near and far—we're organizing a reunion! This is a chance to see your family members, and maybe even meet some new ones. One of the longest-running family gatherings in the United States has been held by the Siler family every year since 1853. There are usually about 250 members of the family who attend.

Reunions are a special way for family members to stay in touch with each other. It's particularly important when they live in different towns, cities, or countries from one another. The largest known reunion took place in 2012, when 4,514 members of the Porteau-Boileve family gathered together in a town in France.

Welcome Family!

Some people are able to trace their family back to an ancestor who lived hundreds of years ago. Queen Elizabeth II of the British royal family is a descendant of one of the first kings of England, Alfred the Great. He reigned in the 9th century, more than 1,000 years ago.

Do you know the stories of any of your ancestors? It might be interesting to find out where they came from and what happened during their lifetimes. Learning more about family members who came before you might also help you discover more about your family today.

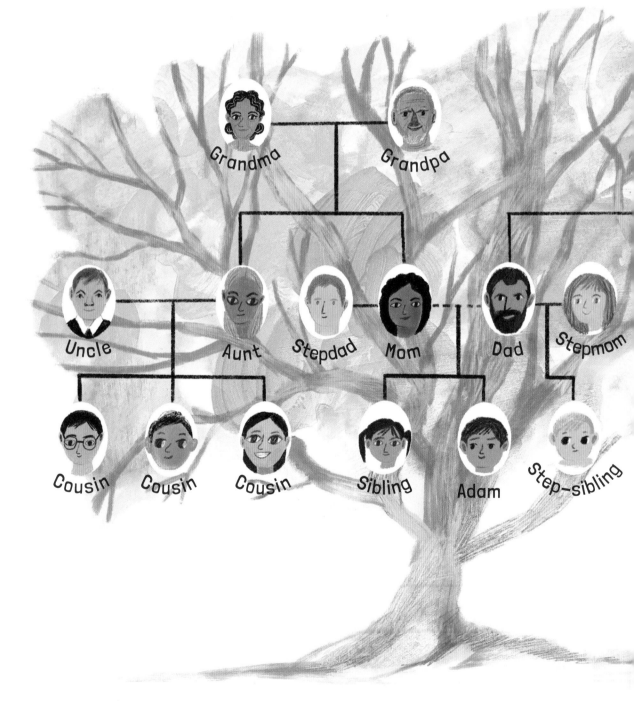

So, how do you learn about your extended family? Creating a family tree is a good place to start. A family tree is a chart that shows how your family members are related. Filling in the tree will help you see how members of your extended family are connected to you.

There are many names for relatives—your siblings might be your brother or sister. Your parent's sibling might be called your aunt, uncle, or your auncle. Your parents' parents could be your grandma, grandpa, grandy, pawpaw, or dozens of other names!

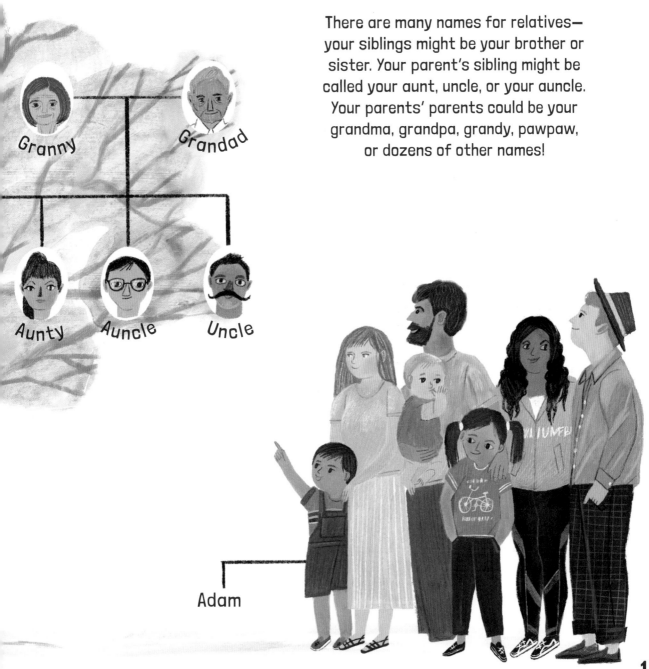

Granny

Grandad

Aunty

Auncle

Uncle

Adam

No matter how big or small, a family reunion is also a great way to celebrate your culture and heritage. One way to do this is to make and eat special food. Certain dishes could be traditional in your family's culture. For example, your family might have a barbecue with an uncle's famous spicy chili sauce. Or you may get to enjoy a grandma's delicious goat curry from a secret recipe handed down through the generations.

Another way to learn about a family's heritage is through language. Many families speak different languages, or they might have different ways of saying things, depending on where they live. For example, in Malta, children call their grandfather *Nannu* (NA-noo), and their grandmother *Nanna* (NA-nah). In Cuba, grandmothers are called *Abuela* (ab-WEY-lah) and grandfathers are called *Abuelo* (ab-WEY-low). In Denmark, your mother's parents would be your *Mormor* (MAW-moah) and *Morfa* (MAW-fah), and your father's parents would be your *Farfar* (FAH-fah) and *Farmor* (FAH-moah). Coming together with all of your family can be a way of finding out who you are and some of the things that make you special.

Game On!

Shall we play a game? Yes! Then gather around and put your game face on. Let's start with something that you can carry in your pocket and can be used to play many different things. Can you guess what it might be? It's a deck of playing cards.

King of Spades

Ace of Spades

Queen of Clubs

Playing cards have existed for a long time. Historians think they were invented in Asia more than 1,000 years ago. A standard, modern deck contains 52 cards divided into four groups called suits. The different suits each have a symbol—hearts, diamonds, spades, or clubs. These suits are numbered between two and ten or given a rank of ace, king, queen, or jack.

The oldest-known complete deck of cards is called the Cloisters Deck. These cards are more than 500 years old and are kept in a museum in New York City. They were hand-drawn, which makes them both rare and valuable. Today, machine printing techniques are used to make the production of cards faster and cheaper.

Cloisters Deck

One card game that you can play with your family is called Snap. There are several ways to play this game, but all of them require a keen eye and quick hands. The aim of the game is to collect as many cards as possible. To play, you divide the deck up by the number of people playing. Each person holds their pile of cards upside down. Then you take turns flipping over your cards onto a central pile. If you spot two cards of the same number or rank, be the first to shout "SNAP," and the cards in the pile are yours. The first person to get all of the cards is the winner.

Playing board games is also an enjoyable way to spend time with family and friends. There are many types of board games from all over the world. One of the oldest is called Mancala.

Mancala boards can be made of stone, wood, or clay, or they can be drawn on the ground or a piece of paper. Some are beautifully carved with animal heads or brightly decorated with paints. Most boards have two rows of holes or spaces in which playing pieces are placed. These pieces might be made from seeds, pebbles, or stones. The goal of this game is simple: capture as many playing pieces as you can while moving your pieces around the board from space to space. The winner is the person with the most pieces at the end of the game.

Mancala has been played across Africa and Asia for thousands of years. There are now many different names for the game and different versions, too. The Maasai people of Tanzania and Kenya often carry a board with them when they are watching over their grazing cattle or goats. It can be a great way to pass the time.

Not all games need special boards or equipment to play. Some games simply need words. Here are two word games that require just some creativity and your thinking cap!

I Went to the Market

Someone starts the game by saying, "I went to the market and bought…an orange."

The next person says the same thing but adds to it. For example, "I went to the market and bought an orange and a blue ball."

Everyone takes a turn and must remember all the items in the order they were said before adding their own item to the shopping list.

The first person to forget an item is out. The last person to remember everything wins!

Would You Rather

In this game, everyone takes a turn asking a question about a made-up scenario. Questions can be as simple as, "Would you rather ski down a steep hill or skate across a frozen lake?" Or they can be totally silly: "Would you rather kiss a shark on the nose or ride piggyback on a bear?" Everyone else gets to answer your question and then make up their own.

Can you make up a game that is played without a board or game pieces? When you've thought of your game, try playing it with your family!

Animal Homes

Like human families, animal families need homes to keep them safe. Animals are very clever at finding all sorts of nooks and crannies to curl up in. And if they can't find a comfy home, they build one!

From the roots to the branches, trees make great homes for many animals. In parts of North America, bright bluebirds weave twigs, leaves, and moss into little basket-like nests. These nests are the perfect places to lay eggs and keep them warm until they're ready to hatch.

Red squirrels like to snuggle up in trees, too. Squirrel nests are called dreys and are often found in holes in tree trunks.

Porcupines feel at home in hollows at the bottom of trees. When a female has baby porcupettes, she sometimes leaves a smelly pile of poop outside to scare other animals away!

Beavers love the water. When two beavers have a family, they build a home called a lodge on a lake or river. Beavers cut down trees by gnawing them with their teeth. Then, they use the wood to create a dam. A dam is a barrier that blocks water and makes a little pond in which the beavers can build their lodge.

A beaver's lodge is a good place to keep beaver babies, called kits, safe and warm. Beavers are such great builders that the biggest beaver dams can be seen from space!

A fallen tree trunk makes a cozy den for a gray fox mother and her babies, which are also called kits. Look closely and you'll see a spider home, too.

A snail never needs to hurry home because home is on its back! Snails carry spiral shells with them wherever they go. They shrink inside whenever danger is near.

Mountains are full of deep, dark caves and winding burrows, which are excellent places to hide away from the wind, rain, and snow.

Take a peek inside a cave in the Rocky Mountains and you might spy hundreds or even thousands of small, winged creatures. These are bats, the only mammals that can fly. By day, these bats huddle together and sleep hanging upside down. But at night, they flit through the sky, searching for juicy insects to eat.

Pumas are purrr-fectly suited to the cooler mountain climate. These powerful cats have thick, yellowy-brown fur to keep them warm. Pumas are most active at nighttime. They have excellent balance and can easily leap from rock to rock. Mothers carry their spotty kittens onto high ledges to keep them safe. From there, the cats can look out for predators.

Meet the marmot, also known as a ground squirrel. Marmots live in mountainous habitats, too. They squeeze in between the gaps in rocks and dig long, underground burrows. It's a good way to avoid the hungry foxes and sharp-eyed golden eagles that might want to eat them. Every now and then, a marmot will sneak a peek outside to check if the coast is clear. Then it will scurry off to find some fresh grass to nibble on.

Would you be happy snoozing on a bed of ice or in a hot, sandy desert? Probably not. But for some hardy creatures, these places are home sweet home.

Antarctica isn't just cold, it's positively frrreeeeeeezing! But that's how penguins like it. Adélie penguins spend most of their lives on floating sea ice, but when the time comes to have chicks, they move onto land in huge numbers and build nests made of stones. Each penguin pair produces two eggs, and the parents take turns keeping them warm. When one penguin parent is caring for the eggs, the other goes fishing for food. Once the chicks are born, the parents keep taking turns. They fish for themselves and also bring back food for their chicks.

The long-legged secretary bird wins the prize for having the prickliest bed. It can take these birds up to six months to build their huge nests in the thorny acacia trees of the African savanna. Their nests are made of twigs, grass, and a bit of fur, held together with dung, which is animal poop. High above the ground the chicks are safe from predators—and they have a great view!

The Mojave Desert in the southwestern United States is home to desert night lizards. These little lizards are unique because they stay with their families instead of living alone. Desert night lizards are also one of the few types of lizard to give birth to live babies instead of laying eggs. When they are born, the babies are usually no larger than a toothpick.

Creepy-crawly Hideaways

Some animal homes are small, cozy places, built for families of three or four. But others are home to hundreds and even thousands of creatures. Welcome to the world of insects! Many creepy-crawlies, including ants, termites, and bees live in groups called colonies, and they build the most incredible homes.

Bee hive

One buzzy little critter that lives in a colony is the honeybee. It lives in a sticky home called a hive that's full of delicious, sweet honey. A hive is made of wax, which bees make inside their bodies.

In the wild, honeybees build their hives in trees and deep cracks in rocks. A hive is just like a busy town, with more than 50,000 bees inside. Each bee has a job to do. Some are builder bees, who fix and repair the hive when cracks appear. Others take care of the babies, which are called larvae. Defender bees scare away unwanted guests and a queen bee produces all the larvae.

The job of worker bees is to pack nectar into honey cells made from wax. These bees beat their tiny wings and create a warm breeze, which turns the nectar into honey. Then, the worker bees seal each little section with fresh wax. In wintertime, honeybees peel off the waxy seal and feast on the honey inside. Yum!

Beekeeper

Apiary

A beekeeper is a person who keeps bees in a wooden beehive called an apiary. Inside, a colony of honeybees builds honeycombs on trays, which the beekeeper collects.

Meet the architects of the insect world: termites. These creatures are tiny, about as small as your pinky fingernail. However, when they work together, they can build the biggest mounds in the insect world.

A large mound takes about four to five years to build and is home to as many as two million termites.

The walls look solid, but they are actually full of tiny holes that let fresh air in and stale air out.

The magnetic termite that is found in Australia builds a unique type of mound. The mounds are tall, thin, and always have one end pointing north. Scientists think that these termites can detect Earth's magnetic field, just like a compass. That's how they are able to position their mound in the right direction to stop it from getting too hot in the midday sun.

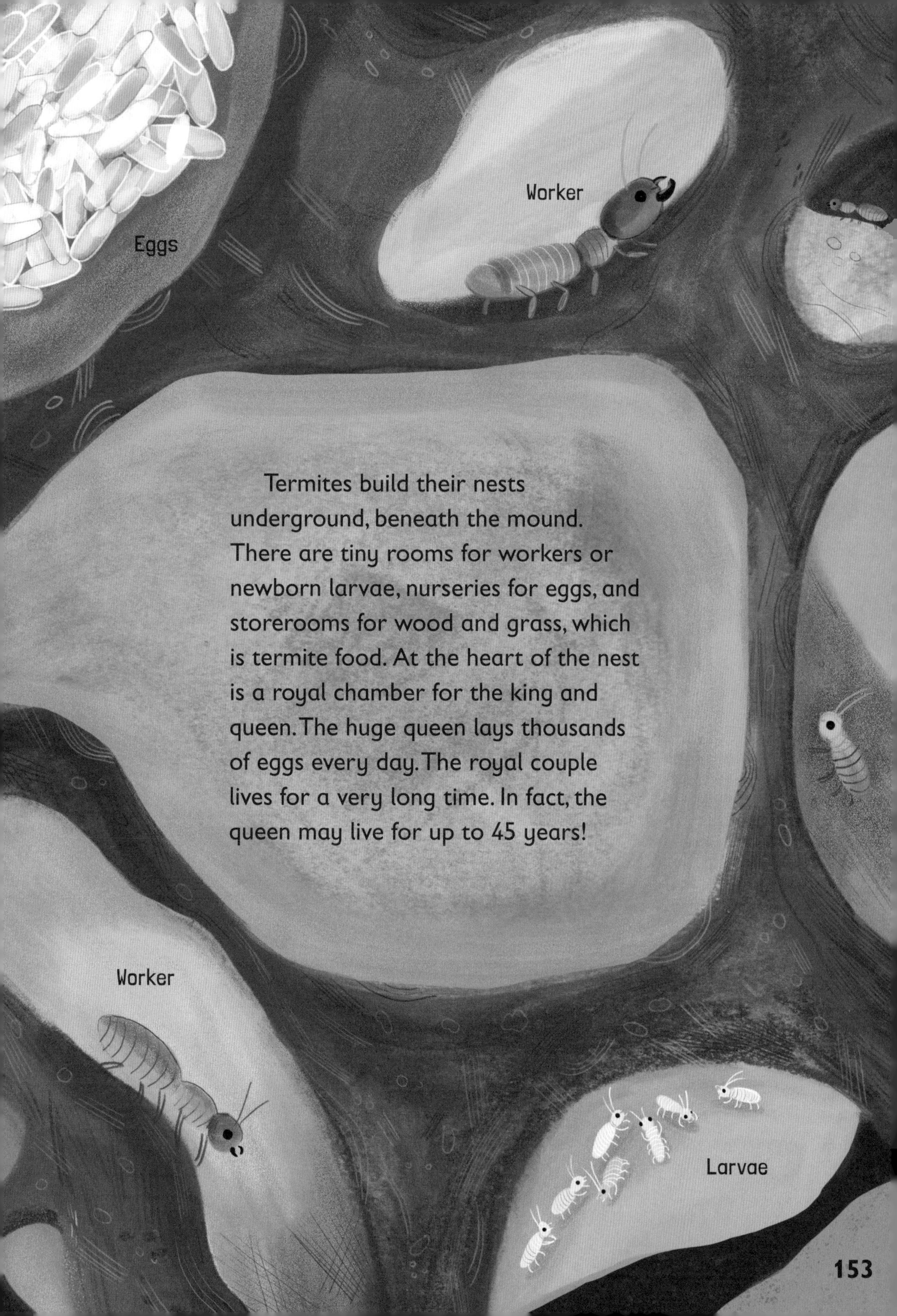

Eggs

Worker

Termites build their nests underground, beneath the mound. There are tiny rooms for workers or newborn larvae, nurseries for eggs, and storerooms for wood and grass, which is termite food. At the heart of the nest is a royal chamber for the king and queen. The huge queen lays thousands of eggs every day. The royal couple lives for a very long time. In fact, the queen may live for up to 45 years!

Worker

Larvae

Deep in the rain forests of South America lives an eight-legged creepy-crawly with a very grand name. Meet *Anelosimus eximius*, or *A. eximius* for short. This rare spider lives in colonies, just like bees and termites. Where you find one of these little spiders, you may find many more—up to 50,000!

A single spider can weave a beautiful web, but imagine what 50,000 spiders can do all together. Colonies of *A. eximius* spiders can weave webs that are bigger than elephants. These webs are mostly full of females and their baby spiderlings, so they're really enormous spider nurseries.

A huge web is handy for catching other creepy-crawlies. Unsuspecting insects crawl, walk, or fly into the sticky web and become trapped—turning into tasty snacks for the spiders.

In 2013, a scientist working in Peru uncovered a different type of teeny tiny spider nursery. It belonged to the so-called Silkhenge spider, and had a mini spire, surrounded by a picket fence made of fine, white spider silk. A couple of golden spiderlings hatched from inside the spire, so scientists think the fence might be a kind of spider playpen. However, scientists don't know whether it was meant to protect the spiderlings, or to trap insects for them to eat!

Water Babies

In the depths of the ocean, millions of little babies are waiting to hatch. Keeping a careful eye on their eggs are some very protective parents. One of these is the octopus. A female octopus can lay as many as 100,000 eggs. Each one looks like a little milky teardrop. The mother doesn't take her eyes off them—not even to find food for herself. When they hatch, her babies are the size of single rice grains, tiny tentacles included.

In the Pacific Ocean, a male Denise's pygmy seahorse curls its tail around the coral. These seahorses are teeny tiny. Adults grow to only about 3/4 inch (2 centimeters) long, so imagine how small the babies are! Unlike most other animals, seahorse dads are the ones that give birth to their young. They have a special pocket called a brood pouch, which can hold up to 34 babies.

Denise's
pygmy
seahorse

Mouthbrooders are a category of animals that have a special way of looking after their young. Can you guess what it is? They carry their eggs in their mouths! The male yellow-headed jawfish is one such creature. After a female lays her eggs, the male scoops them up and holds them in his mouth until they are ready to hatch.

There are three seahorses in the coral below. Can you spot them?

The biggest baby on Earth belongs to the gigantic blue whale. When these babies are born, they can weigh as much as an adult Asian elephant. Baby whales are called calves, and they feed on their mother's milk. A calf may gain up to 200 pounds (90 kilograms) a day from milk alone. That's the weight of 25 bowling balls! Despite their big size, calves swim near their mothers, fins gently touching, for comfort and protection.

The ocean is a dangerous place if you don't know how to stay safe. Luckily, baby dolphins have very smart moms to teach them the rules. Young dolphins can swim as soon as they are born, but their mothers will push them up to the surface to take their first breath of air. Babies are also taught some clever hunting techniques. Off the coast of Australia, bottlenose dolphins have been seen with sea sponges on the ends of their noses. This is a clever trick that protects their beaks from the rough sand when they are looking for food on the ocean floor.

The Galápagos sea lion lives on land and in the water. It can clamber up rocks, gallop across a beach, and swim underwater like a graceful acrobat. Young sea lion pups are raised in ready-made nursery pools on the beach called rookeries. Here, the pups splash and play while staying safe from danger. When female sea lions are hungry, they leave their pups playing in the pools, knowing they're being looked after by the other moms.

Another animal that spends its time on land and in water is the crocodile. These reptiles have one of the most powerful bites in the animal kingdom, but when it comes to looking after their babies, they're as gentle as can be. When a mother hears little squeaks coming from her sandy nest, she carefully gathers her hatchlings into her jaws and carries them to the water's edge for their first swim.

Whether they are big or small, live in freshwater or salt water, all of these water babies have a strong start in life with a little help from their families.

Animal Mealtimes

When it comes to mealtimes, lots of baby animals fend for themselves from day one. But there are plenty of creatures that rely on mom and dad to bring them food.

The golden lion tamarin is a rare little monkey that lives in a small area of forest in Brazil. Tamarin babies are often born in pairs, and feed on their mother's milk for the first few weeks after they're born. The dad also helps out as the babies grow. A father tamarin will take his babies into the jungle to find food. Sometimes the babies hitch a ride by clinging to their dad's fur. Other times, they follow behind.

Red foxes are devoted parents. Their babies are called kits, and when they are born, they are blind, deaf, and toothless. The female, called a vixen, stays with her kits for weeks on end, never leaving them. The male fox brings her meals every day. When the kits are a few months old, their parents bury meat close to the family den to teach the youngsters how to hunt and dig for food.

The top prize for being a dedicated dad goes to the long-legged, male rhea bird. This dad builds a nest in which to keep the eggs. When they hatch, the dad may find himself in charge of dozens of chicks, which he takes care of for up to six months. That's a lot of beaks to feed! Dad teaches his chicks which seeds, leaves, and shoots to eat, and where to find chewy insects, so they can start feeding themselves.

It's not always easy for animal parents to feed their babies. A sea otter mom has to eat an enormous amount so that she can make milk for her pups. This means she often has to leave her pups alone in the water to go fishing. But, there's an issue—newborn pups can't swim!

No problem! Mom has a clever way of making sure her pups stay safe while she's away. She fluffs up their fur to trap air inside so they float. Then, she wraps them up in sea kelp so they don't drift off. Sea otters have the thickest fur of any mammal. When the babies are all fluffed up and secure, mom will leave them bobbing on the surface while she dives down for crabs, mussels, or spiny sea urchins to feast on.

When it comes to teamwork, flamingos know how it's done. These orangey-pink birds live in colonies of thousands, and males and females often stay together for life. They build their nest in a shallow lake, and after the female lays an egg, both parents share in the egg-warming duties.

When the hatchlings are born, mom and dad are both on hand for mealtimes. Flamingo parents feed their young a substance called "crop milk." When a hungry chick begs for food, the parents produce crop milk in their tummies, bring it up, and pass it to the open beak of the hungry chick. Flamingos do this until their chicks are old enough to feed themselves. At this point, the chicks start eating algae and tiny shrimp. These foods are rich in a red-orange substance called beta-carotene, which gives flamingos their beautiful color.

Epic Animal Journeys

There are some animal families that spend all their lives in one place. And there are others that go on epic journeys called migrations, crossing continents or even oceans on their extraordinary travels.

The northernmost parts of Earth are bitterly cold and icy, but it's the perfect place for caribou. These animals live in huge herds, and in spring, as many as 500,000 of them make a long trek south to summer feeding grounds. Caribou travel up to 930 miles (1,500 kilometers), which is about the same as the distance between New York State and Mississippi. When they arrive, the females give birth. The newborn calves munch on the lush grass and quickly grow larger.

When summer ends, the herd begins the journey back to the winter grounds. The calves wobble on long legs, staying close to their mothers for protection.

Caribou and reindeer look the same and both belong to the same species, or group, of animals. However, they are found in different parts of the world. Caribou live in North America, whereas reindeer live in northern Europe and Asia.

Where there are caribou, there are sure to be gray wolves to hunt them. Caribou are fast, so the wolves must be sneaky if they want to catch one for a meal. If they startle the herd, the wolves will struggle to catch them. A pair of wolves leads the pack, often tracking the herd of caribou for days on end.

In the grasslands and deserts of Mongolia, two-humped Bactrian camels travel far and wide to find food and water. Up to 30 females and their calves are led by a large, shaggy-haired male. Together, they are known as a caravan of camels. Water is scarce in the desert and the camels plod on for days without a drink. They can last for weeks without food, too. This is possible because camels store fat in their humps. When there is nothing to eat, their bodies turn the fat into food. Life in the Mongolian desert is harsh, so calves stay with their mothers for about three years, learning how to survive.

Another migratory animal that is also found in Mongolia, as well as farther west in Central Asia, is the saiga, a type of antelope. They have soft brown fur, long legs, and horns. Below the saiga's eyes sits a huge, wobbly nose that's similar to an elephant's trunk, but shorter. In winter, the saiga's nose warms the freezing cold air as it's breathed in. And in summer, its nose filters out dust kicked up by the traveling herd when it's on the move. A saiga herd travels about 620 miles (1,000 kilometers) to find breeding grounds rich in green grass for their calves to eat.

Perhaps the most incredible journeys of all happen in the air. Come wintertime, flocks of migrating birds make extremely long journeys to find food and a warm place to nest. It's up to the grown-ups to show young chicks the way.

The high-flying champions of the world are bar-headed geese. They fly in a "V" shape in family groups or colonies. Every year, they travel from their nesting grounds in Mongolia and China all the way to India. They cross the Himalayas, the highest mountains on Earth. Some geese even soar to dizzying heights of 23,000 feet (7,000 meters) or more. It's hard work flying at the front of the V, so adult geese take turns leading the flock.

The record for the longest nonstop flight is held by the bar-tailed godwit. Males and females raise their chicks together in the northernmost parts of the world, such as Alaska. When the weather turns cold, these long-legged birds fly the length of the Pacific Ocean to New Zealand, where it's summertime. They can cover up to 7,500 miles (12,000 kilometers) in just over one week. That's more than a quarter of the way around the world! When the godwits arrive, they're skinny, hungry, and very thirsty. The flocks enjoy the warm summer before flying north again to breed during the summer months there.

Work First, Then Play

Animals who live in a group enjoy all sorts of benefits, and they will often work, rest, and play together. When a group of animals hunts together, they have a better chance of catching dinner, which the group can share. This means that no one goes hungry. It is also safer for many animals to live in groups, as there are many more eyes to watch for predators.

On the grasslands of East Africa, African wild dogs become a flash of black, tan, and white fur as they sprint toward their pack. Wild dogs love the company of other dogs, and there's lots of yelping and excitement when they're together. When it's time for work, the dogs fan out to hunt for lunch. A gazelle would be a great catch…

When the sun is high in the sky, it's time to rest. On a grassy mound, lions stretch out and lick their fur after the early morning hunt. Lions are the most sociable of all wild cats. The proud males rub heads with each other to show that they're friends. Lionesses nuzzle and lick each other to show affection.

Over by the watering hole, a group of stripy zebras, known as a dazzle, keeps a watchful eye. They whinny, bark, and snort to warn each other that lions and African wild dogs are on the prowl, and that they might have to sprint away. If they do, zebras have speed on their side—they can run up to 40 miles per hour (65 kilometers per hour).

175

Once dinner is over, it's time to play. Lively games are good for animals in lots of ways. When animals race around, climb, and play catch, the exercise helps their muscles grow stronger.

Black bears live in North America. Adult bears usually like to live alone, but cubs stay with their mothers for the first 18 months of their lives. Cubs have a lot to learn about the forest, and they love to play. Whether it's tree climbing, rolling in shallow streams, or chasing each other until they're worn out, playing helps bear cubs learn the skills that they need to survive when they are adults.

Birds like to play too—especially magpies, crows, and ravens. When teenage ravens leave their parents, they hang out together in gangs. They chase each other through the air and drop sticks for each other to catch. This helps to strengthen their wings and makes them faster fliers.

Baby elephants feel safe beside their mothers, but when another elephant calf wants to play, the temptation to leave her can be hard to resist. The calves race around, ears flapping and trunks trumpeting, until they land in a big gray heap on the ground, tired and ready for a nap.

It's early morning in Central Africa. A warm mist is rising, and a troop of 60 chimpanzees is about to start their day. Chimps love hanging out together. Females pick leaves and share sweet fruit, while looking after their new babies or keeping an eye on the older children.

Older chimps are well respected in the troop. They teach youngsters how to groom, which is very important because it keeps their fur clean and free of pesky insects.

A few adult males patrol the boundary of the troop's territory. It's their job to scare off any unwanted visitors. If a rival troop comes prowling, the males grunt and roar to scare them away.

The younger chimps have lots to keep them busy. If they're not poking an ants' nest with a stick, they like to climb trees, swing from branch to branch, and hang upside down together. Chimpanzees are closely related to humans. Like many people, they're happy working together and playing together, chattering all the while.

Dinosaur Families and More

Millions of years ago, Earth was a very different place, and dinosaurs large and small roamed the land. As parents, these ancient creatures weren't so different from the crocodiles and birds that live today. They built nests, laid eggs, and looked after their young.

We can learn a lot about dinosaurs and other ancient creatures by studying fossils. Fossils are the preserved remains or impressions of animals or plants. One of the most interesting dinosaur fossils ever found was a fossilized nest. It belonged to a *Maiasaura*, which means "good mother lizard." This duck-billed dinosaur laid its eggs in hollows in the mud. Scientists believed that after they hatched, the mother would fetch plants for the hatchlings to eat. She would watch over them until they were strong enough to find their own food.

Though fossils give us clues about dinosaurs, sometimes those clues are hard to understand. This was the case with a dinosaur that was known as *Oviraptor*, which means "egg snatcher." In the 1920s, scientists found a fossilized nest of dinosaur eggs, with an adult dinosaur on top. The dinosaur had a razor-sharp beak, which made the scientists think that it had died trying to eat the eggs. However, after the discovery of another nest in the 1990s, the truth was revealed. The eggs actually belonged to the *Oviraptor*. The dinosaur was a mother or father who had died on the nest, protecting its young from a sandstorm.

For many dinosaurs, looking after their babies meant staying alert. Hungry meat-eaters often lurked near nesting sites, waiting for the right moment to snatch a hatchling or a young dinosaur taking its first steps. When it came to protecting their babies, dinosaur mothers and fathers did not back down without a fight.

Protoceratops was a small dinosaur that lived in herds in dry, windswept deserts where Mongolia is today. Females laid their eggs and looked after their young in sandy nests. Both *Protoceratops* parents kept watch for *Velociraptor*, the "quick thief," who would try to grab an egg or a baby. If *Velociraptor* came hunting, it would likely get a nasty nip from the sharp beak of a *Protoceratops*.

Chasmosauruses had long, pointy horns and big frills which they used to protect their babies. Scientists think that when they felt threatened, *Chasmosauruses* might have formed a tight circle around their young, facing outward. This position would likely scare away any other dinosaurs that came looking for a quick bite.

While dinosaurs roamed Earth, other ancient reptiles called pterosaurs dominated the skies. They came in all shapes and sizes. Some pterosaurs were as tiny as sparrows, while others measured 39 feet (12 meters) from wingtip to wingtip. That's almost as long as a bus!

Many of these flying reptiles lived by the sea and ate fish. In China, scientists discovered the fossils of a long-snouted, toothy pterosaur with a huge clutch of more than 200 eggs. This seemed like a lot of eggs for just one female, so scientists figured out that this pterosaur must have nested in large colonies, where many females laid eggs near each other.

In Brazil, scientists found the fossils of another type of pterosaur. The babies seemed to have strong wing bones, similar to the ones found in the adults. This made the scientists think that the young may have been able to fly soon after they hatched. Scientists nicknamed the baby pterosaurs "flaplings." Experts also think these pterosaurs may have stayed together in colonies for their whole lives.

Many prehistoric parents worked hard to protect their young from the dangers around them. In doing so, they gave their babies the best chance of survival, so that they could grow up and have families of their own.

Meet the Authors & Illustrators

We are very grateful to all the authors and illustrators who have brightened these pages with their illuminating stories and pictures.

AUTHORS

Alli Brydon is a children's book author and lifelong New Yorker who moved to the South of England with her family in 2018. She loves to draw and dreams about illustrating children's books one day. Her favorite place is the beach, but the mountains constantly call to her. Alli has the sense of humor of a seven-year-old. And she will never ever kill a spider. *Alli's stories: "No Place Like Home," "The Great Outdoors," "The Wonder of Trees," "Pedal Power," and "It's Vacation Time."*

Catherine D. Hughes researched, wrote, and edited for National Geographic children's magazines and books during her 35-year career there. She retired as the Executive Editor of Preschool Content. Catherine continues to write children's non-fiction, specializing in natural history and science. Her books include several titles in National Geographic's *Little Kids First Big Book* series. She lives in Alexandria, Virginia. *Catherine's stories: "What's for Breakfast?," "Staying Clean," "Mind Your Manners," "Cleaning Up," "Storytime," "Animals in the Family," "Fun at the Playground," "Camping Adventures," "Splashing Around,"* *"Let's Go Shopping!," "Up, Down, Round and Round," "Happy Birthday to You!," "Growing Families," "Getting Married," "Saying Farewell," "Let's Celebrate!," "Family Reunions," and "Game On!"*

Jackie McCann has worked in children's publishing for many years and is an experienced writer and editor. She specializes in children's non-fiction and works with brilliant authors, illustrators, and designers to create children's novelty books. *Jackie's stories: "Animal Homes," "Creepy-crawly Hideaways," "Water Babies," "Animal Mealtimes," "Epic Animal Journeys," "Work First, Then Play," and "Dinosaur Families and More."*

ILLUSTRATORS

Anneli Bray is a children's illustrator living in the north west of England. She is known for her warm, colorful illustrations influenced by her love of animals (her favorites are foxes), nature, and a longing for adventure. *Anneli illustrated pages 144–185.*

Vivian Mineker is a Taiwanese-American illustrator currently based in Ljubljana, Slovenia. She's always loved to create images that bring to life the imaginative world she's constantly daydreaming of. She mainly uses watercolor and gouache as the traditional part of her work, then puts on the finishing touches digitally with Photoshop. *Vivian illustrated the cover and pages 54–101.*

Sofia Moore is a Ukrainian-American artist and illustrator based in Las Vegas, Nevada. She grew up reading folk tales in her grandmother's house and drawing princesses on the backs of textbooks. Now she is on a mission to create her own picture books filled with colorful characters and imaginary situations. She loves painting traditionally, and layers textures both on paper and digitally. *Sofia illustrated pages 102–143.*

Skylar White is an illustrator living in New York City with her husband and their cat, Alfie. Prior to New York, she lived in Denver, Colorado, and got her degree in illustration from the Rocky Mountain College of Art and Design. She has an affinity for projects that infuse the everyday with a touch of the magical and absurd. Her preferred media are watercolor and gouache. *Skylar illustrated pages 6–53.*

Glossary

algae: a plant or plant-like organism that usually lives in water

ancestor: a person who was in someone's family in the past, or an animal from the past, from which a modern animal developed

ancient: very old

appliance: a machine (such as an oven, microwave, or dishwasher) that is powered by electricity and that is used in people's homes to perform a particular job

architect: a person who designs buildings

body language: movements or positions of the body that express a person's thoughts or feelings

bungalow: a house that has one or one and a half stories and often a front porch

carbon dioxide: a gas that is produced when animals (including humans) breathe out, or when certain fuels (such as gasoline) are burned. It is used by plants for energy

climate: the general weather conditions over a long time in a particular area

compost: a decaying mixture of organic matter (such as leaves and grass) that is used to improve the soil in a garden

concrete: a hard, strong material that is used for building, and is made by mixing cement, sand, and broken rocks with water

culture: the beliefs or customs of a particular society, group, place, or time

delta: a piece of land shaped like a triangle that is formed when a river splits into smaller streams before it flows into the ocean

gravity: a natural force that causes all physical things in the universe to move toward one another, for example, causing objects to fall toward the Earth.

heritage: the beliefs and traditions that are part of the history of a particular group of people

microscope: a device used for producing a much larger view of very small objects so that they can be seen clearly

migration: the movement from one country or place to another for a period of time

molecule: the smallest possible amount of a particular substance

nutritious: having substances that a person or animal needs to be healthy and grow properly

organism: an individual living thing

oxygen: a chemical that is found in the air, that has no color, taste, or smell and that animals (including humans) need to breathe to stay alive

pollute: to make something dirty and not safe or suitable to use

predator: an animal that lives by killing and eating other animals

recycle: to turn something old into something new

sociable: liking to be in the company of other people or animals

symbolize: to represent or express something through the use of symbols

tapestry: a heavy cloth that has designs or pictures woven into it

technique: a way of doing something by using specialist knowledge or skill

tortilla: a round, thin bread that was first developed in Mexico and Central America

tradition: a way of thinking, behaving, or doing something that has been used by the people in a particular group, family, or society for a long time

Definitions courtesy of Merriam-Webster.

Sources

All the pages in this book have been fact-checked by the team at **Britannica**, and the authors have drawn from the articles on britannica.com in their research. They have also consulted numerous other publications and articles, and would like to acknowledge the following key sources in the making of this book:

WEBSITES

www.bbc.co.uk

www.dkfindout.com

www.emilypost.com/advice/top-table-manners-for-kids

www.guinnessworldrecords.com

www.konmari.com

www.nationalgeographic.com

www.nhm.ac.uk

www.scholastic.com

www.smithsonianmag.com

www.time.com/5259602/japanese-forest-bathing

BOOKS

Brooke, Michael, and Birkhead, Tim, *Cambridge Encyclopedia of Ornithology* (Cambridge University Press, 1991)

Jenkins, Dr. Ian, *The Explorer's Book of Dinosaurs* (Two-Can Publishing, 2000)

Newman, Aline Alexander, and Weitzman, Gary, *How to Speak Dog: A Guide to Decoding Dog Language* (National Geographic Kids Books, 2013)

Newman, Aline Alexander, and Weitzman, Gary, *How to Speak Cat: A Guide to Decoding Cat Language* (National Geographic Kids Books, 2015)

Index

**BRITANNICA
BOOKS**

Britannica Books is an imprint of What on Earth Publishing, published in collaboration with Britannica, Inc.
Allington Castle, Maidstone, Kent ME16 0NB, United Kingdom
30 Ridge Road Unit B, Greenbelt, Maryland, 20770, United States

First published in the United States in 2022

Text by Alli Brydon, Catherine D. Hughes, and Jackie McCann
Design and Art Direction by Kim Hankinson
Cover design by Andy Forshaw and Kim Hankinson
Cover illustration by Vivian Mineker
Illustrations by Anneli Bray, Vivian Mineker, Sofia Moore, and Skylar White
Index by Helen Peters
Book production and print production by Booklabs.co.uk

Encyclopaedia Britannica
Alison Eldridge, Managing Editor; Michele Rita Metych, Fact Checking Supervisor.

Britannica Books
Nancy Feresten, Publisher; Natalie Bellos, Executive Editor; Andy Forshaw, Art Director;
Katy Lennon, Editor; Meg Osborne, Assistant Editor.

With special thanks to Adriana Cloud, Angela Sangma Francis,
Priyanka Lamichhane and Joanna Micklem.

Library of Congress Cataloging-in-Publication Data available upon request.

ISBN: 9781913750381

RP/Haryana, India/08/2021

Printed and bound in India

10 9 8 7 6 5 4 3 2 1

www.whatonearthbooks.com

Think. Seek.
Play. Learn.
Britannica.

Your family's key to discovering the
amazingly weird and strangely true.

Or visit
premium.britannica.com/learn